Blood & Bone
Remember

Blood & Bone Remember

Poems from Appalachia by
Jane Hicks

Jane Hicks

With an Introduction by
Silas House

Jesse Stuart Foundation
Ashland, Ky
2005

Acknowledgments & Special Thanks

The author wishes to thank the editors of the
following publications where these poems originally appeared:

A! Magazine: Phototropism.
Appalachian Heritage: Packhorse Librarian, To My Welsh Ancestors,
   My Mother's Trunk, Winter Garden, Paradise Regained, Ancestral Home.
Appalachian Journal: Come October, Deep Winter.
Now and Then: Diamond Jenny #4: Mistress Mine, Finding Herself in
   Knoxville TN on a Non-football Saturday the Cosmic Possum Visits a
   Poetry Slum, Sestina for Second Semester, Songcatcher, Raising the Nap,
   Felix Culpa
Iron Mountain Review: Where You From, Honey?
Pine Mountain Sand and Gravel: Diamond Jenny #1
Red Crow Poetry Review: Diamond Jenny #7
Sow's Ear: Diamond Jenny #2: Going Home
Wind: How We Became Cosmic Possums, Remnants
Now & Then Appalachian Poetry Competition 2002: Felix culpa (1st prize)
Tennessee Mountain Writers 2002: First Day Photo (3rd prize)
James Still Award for Poetry, Appalachian Writers' Association: Deep
   Winter (1st prize, 2003), Come October, (2nd prize, 2001)
Bob Snyder Poetry Prize 2001: Diamond Jenny #7 (honorable mention)
Now & Then Poetry Contest 2000: Raising the Nap (honorable mention)
Literary Lunch: Knoxville Writers Guild Anthology: Huckleberries, Apple
   Butter Psalm
Migrants and Stowaways: Knoxville Writers Guild Anthology: Chronology of
   a Dreamer

Poetry and excerpts in novels:
Ancestral Home (excerpt): frontispiece, *Clay's Quilt*, by Silas House,
   Algonquin 2001
First Day Photo: frontispiece, *Plant Life*, by Pamela Duncan 2002
Ancestral Home: frontispiece, *Coal Tattoo* by Silas House, Algonquin 2004

ISBN: 1-931672-31-8

Published By:
Jesse Stuart Foundation
P.O. Box 669 • Ashland, KY 41105
(606) 326-1667 • JSFBOOKS.com

cover art quietly by Jane Hicks

Blood & Bone Remember

Diamond Jenny

Cosmic Possum

Daughters of Necessity

Cassandra

Thalia

Lydia

Introduction

Many people have wondered aloud why Appalachians have such a strong sense of place. I believe the land defines us so much because it has played such a central role in our heritage. The land dictates the lives of Appalachians, effecting everything, whether it be the economy, the kind of food they eat, or the dialect. The best writers—Appalachian or not—know this. They know that the land gets under your skin and takes up residence. In short, the place becomes a part of the person.

Jane Hicks is an Appalachian writer who has always known how important place is to her as a writer and as a human being. When I think of Hicks' poetry, those are the two things that always come immediately to mind: place and humanity. Both themes inform all of her work. Even the title of this collection is a testament to her attention to place and the way place becomes a part of its inhabitants. The title comes from her poem "Ancestral Home," which I find to be one of the major contemporary Appalachian poems. "Blood and bone remember/surely as nerve and neuron," Hicks writes. She speaks of "ghost pain," memory that "calls," even an "elemental reckoning." Hicks is focusing our attention here on the Jungian idea of "collective memory," the theory that all family—or even human—history is stored in our DNA and passed onto us at birth.

Besides drawing our attention to the importance of history and heritage, Hicks also suffuses this poem with imagery that paints a lovely picture of Appalachia. There are "sharp, sweet spring wells," "redbuds weeping thaw," streams that "merge in churning unity." Hicks' poetry causes snapshots to explode in our minds as we read the perfectly-chosen words. We can see those redbuds dripping their thaw, the confluence of creeks, the springs bursting out of the hillsides. With this one poem and the others that make up this beautiful collection, Hicks not only gets to the heart of the matter about what it means to be an Appalachian, but what it means to be alive and walking around with history joining blood to course through our veins. In Hicks' poetry, history is as important as blood, if not more so.

Hicks uses the land in every way to tell stories in her poetry. Witness just one of the characters who are made flesh in her poem about a family that is imploding in "The Fall of the House":

> Three days absent, he smells of smoke, perfume
> and something wild I cannot name, something old like
> blue mud along the creek where crawfish mound
> their homes and ferns drop spores on leaf litter.

In "Gathering of the Clan," Hicks takes us to a family reunion where clogging is accompanied by biscuits that are smeared with "light molasses and blackberry jam/fresh from July picking." In the first section of this collection she also takes us to a hog killing, a session of huckleberry-picking, a country burial, and a revival. She allows us to tag along with Cecil Sharp as he catches the ballads of the region. We bear witness to a young girl who gathers all of her strength to pull a shotgun on her abusive father. When another young girl faces her first day of school, we know that sense of trepidation and mourn with her at the loss of her "battered Agatha Christie, her summer best friend." We travel with Hicks to Appalachia's largest waterfall, to a high school reunion where the former students are still living with Vietnam, to Memphis' Beale Street, and all the way to Texas, where she journeys without ever leaving her beloved mountains far behind. Born and raised in East Tennessee, Hicks has lived her whole life in the mountains she knows as well as the topography of her grandmother's quilts. She has traveled throughout the nation but has lived outside of Appalachia only briefly, most notably in a four month-long jaunt to Minnesota, where her homesickness was so thick that it made her understand her native land at an even deeper level.

This well-traveled sense of adventure leads us right to Hicks' most beloved character, The Cosmic Possum. After her first Cosmic Possum poem—"First Generation Bachelor of Arts" appeared in *Now and Then* in 1986, and its follow-up "How I Became a Cosmic Possum" was published in *Wind* in 1998, Hicks gained a cult following that very few poets ever have. Her website became clogged with visitors and fans started sending her possum cards, possum stuffed animals, and their own possum stories. The Cosmic Possum poems addressed the experience that many people of Hicks' generation have had: they were the first high school and college graduates in their families and while they completely respected their heritage, they also embraced the possibilities of progress that were flowing into the region. According to Hicks, "We had a foot in both worlds," and this is expressed eloquently in "How We Became Cosmic Possums":

> Caught between Country Club and 4-H,
> Neither shrimp nor crawdad,
> Neither hip nor hillbilly,
> Neither feedsack nor cashmere.

These lines also sum up the Jane Hicks I first met in 1997 at the Hindman Settlement School's Appalachian Writer's Conference. I had just finished my first novel and since one of my main characters was a quilter, I was anxious to meet Hicks. She was well-known at the conference not only as an amazing poet, but also as a talented quilter. Upon our first conversation I knew that I had met long-lost kin. That same Appalachian mix of blood and history coursed through both of our veins. Right away I saw that Hicks was not only a magical person of exceptional perception and insight, but also someone whose poetry spoke to me in a way that only James Still's and Ron Rash's did. Her quilts were poems in their own right, each stitch a carefully-chosen word that perfectly completed a bed-size sentence. But as wonderful as her fabric work was, it was really her way with words that stunned me and inspired me so much that I was able to revise my novel and make it better. When the book was published four years later I sent my editor several of Hicks' poems to better acquaint her with the region and the people I was writing about. It didn't take us long to realize that we had to use an excerpt from "Ancestral Home" in the frontispiece to the novel.

I do not claim to be an expert in poetry. I know nothing of rhyme schemes and line breaks and the technicalities of poetry. I can, however, recognize a wonderful poem when I see one. To my mind, a poem should capture one moment in the most beautiful and economic way that it can be pinned down on paper. A poem must be a perfect gathering of words, a small space embodied by all the right images and phrases that convey a picture that can play out in our minds. Therein lies the great attraction to Hicks' poetry. It is accessible. Yes, it is smart, multilayered, and full of symbolism. Her poems are full of images and phrases that prod the reader to go deeper, to mine the rich veins of each poem for all that it offers. But more than all that, great poetry speaks to the reader, and that's exactly what Hicks' poetry does. These poems move us, make us come to a moment of realization. Like the work of Don West or

James Still or Robert Morgan, Hick's poetry speaks to working class people as easily as scholars. Just like Hicks' Cosmic Possum character, her poetry has a foot in both worlds and is enjoyable for anyone who encounters it.

I am not alone among writers in my admiration for Hicks' poetry. Pamela Duncan, the author of such beloved novels as *Moon Women* and *Plant Life*, was so moved by Hicks' "First Day Photo" that she insisted her publishers use the entire poem to begin her novel. "That poem spoke for my characters in a way that I couldn't," Duncan says. "It so perfectly captures a young girl's passion for books and learning, her longing for and expectation of a better life, as well as her acknowledgement of and determination to overcome the many obstacles in her way. Part of my novel *Plant Life* grew out of trying to imagine one possible future for this brave and vulnerable little girl." Sharyn McCrumb, author of the bestselling Ballad Books, says "there is no measure to the influence of" Hicks' poetry on her own work. "I am in awe of her," McCrumb says. In her 2002 novel *The Songcatcher*, McCrumb even named one of her characters the Cosmic Possum and allowed him to spout some of Hicks' wisdom. Besides these well-known names, Hicks has influenced, encouraged, and touched the lives and the writings of countless others during her time at writers' workshops throughout the region and throughout her 27-year career as a teacher and counselor in the public school systems of her native East Tennessee. Young poets at Hindman's annual conference seek her out for her keen eye and unabashed honesty while students she taught more than twenty years ago keep in touch with her for her advice and encouragement.

More than anything, Hicks is a poet who shows Appalachia as a complex place. Her Appalachia is both gritty and beautiful. It is a real place, burdened with neither romanticism or utter despair. Hicks's terrain is a place where strong women muster that strength to defend themselves, a place where berry-picking and books can and do go together. In "Chronology of a Dreamer," she writes, "Stuck a book in my bucket those/hot berry picking days…" and we know that we are in true Appalachia, a place of complexity and the universal need for knowledge, not the stereotypical place—so often seen—where illiteracy is the norm and bib-overalled hillbillies loll around on the crumbling porch, too lazy to unburden the berry brambles of their load.

Likewise, Hicks' series of "Diamond Jenny" poems shed new light on the coal mining experience, observing this particular world through the eyes of fresh new observers like a miner's child, an outsider, or a county agent. These poems neither romanticize nor paint black the practice of coal mining. Instead, they throb with an emotional truth in each one, as when a coal miner's wife awaits news of her husband's death:

> I listened, hearing only
> boot heavy steps,
> a messenger marching
> in time to the death bell
> from the mine mouth
> tolling casualties,
> deep in Kentucky mud.

Later a child is trying to understand her grief for the loss of her father to the mines by studying the burial places of ancient Egyptians but is snapped back to attention by her unsympathetic teacher:

> So I forgot the pyramid.
> That picture still comes to mind
> When I look at the big, granite mountain
> That swallowed my father.

Hicks' "Daughters of Necessity" poems are inspired by the three lovely daughters of Zeus and Themis, women who have the awesome power of controlling the lives of all mortal mankind. The reader does not have to know Greek mythology to understand the power of these poems, but Hicks' attention to the cyclical nature of mythology and its effect on our storytelling tradition gives these poems a mythic quality of their own. Hicks' "Fates" are Cassandra, Thalia, and Lydia, and they are the epitome of strong Appalachian women who are in control of every situation, women who are determined, sexual, smart, and completely alive. In "Felix culpa" Cassandra reacts to the local preacher's condemnation of her child's illegitimate birth this way: "Preacher calls me Magdalene. I refute/him, knowing her wiser in her choosing,/blessed by loving, not damned." Thalia, a pack-horse librarian, is equally independent as she makes her way across the mountains, intent on her mission of getting books to the people. Still the land is always present, always a pulsing force as she moves through a world of "a faint fingernail of moon," a place where redbuds "riot," and where eventually the morning opens up to a sky that "bleeds across the ridge." We are with the third Fate, Lydia, from her first day of fifth grade until she is fifty years old, when she finds herself stitching a quilt that is her "plot for winter." Lydia brings our attention back to quilts, and most of all the many women who "fashioned their castoffs/into naïve art." Lydia has been raised in a society of quilters, women who make art with their hands, and she is glad for this heritage:

> I feel the Fates measure me each time I cut,
> pull out minute stitches they would not approve,
> hear them murmur in the whisper
> of needles through cotton.

Once again we are reminded of our history and its importance. Perhaps more than any other place, Appalachia is a region where its inhabitants must remain aware of its rocky, storied past while also keeping an eye on the jagged horizon. While reading these poems we are to understand the history of ourselves, of a place, and of how those two things are not only forever joined but also dependent upon one another.

The joining of history and heritage, the old ways and the new, and even blood and bone's eternal memory are essential elements in the poetry of Jane Hicks, a poet who possesses not only remarkable skill but also a touch of magic. In her poem "Double Wedding Ring" she tells us of a quilt that is made up of "patches, pieces, remnants, remains" that eventually "join in a testament/to skill and love." This is just what Hicks has given to us in this wonderful debut. I am proud to introduce her work to you. By doing so I feel as if I have been given the opportunity to present a wonderful gift to all those who are willing to receive her words, as well-stitched and sturdy and beautiful as the quilts that show up in this collection.

Silas House
26 July 2004
Hindman, Kentucky

Blood & Bone Remember

Where You From, Honey?

(my answer upon explaining my accent)
for George Ella Lyon

I am from the quilts I sew.
Up from under grandmother's frame
where I played as a toddler,
to the first crooked stitches
she let me sew near the corner.

I am from the counterpanes
spread by an Irish serving girl
over her lady's soft bed.
I am from the scraps of immigrants
pieced into the pattern of me.

English, Irish, Scots, and Welsh
pulled my threads up from the South,
down the wide valley,
through the Gap, up the mountains,
a Celtic knot on a Log Cabin Quilt.

Ancestral Home
(Henry Monteith 1733-1838)

Blood and bone remember
surely as nerve and neuron.
Sharp, sweet spring wells,
eddies through generations.

Redbuds weeping thaw
for blood and bone born
too soon, lying cold.
Sharp, sweet spring a cradle.

Blood and bone left
at fierce Shiloh, heaped
in sharp, sweet, spring.
Ghost pain—memory calls.

Blood and bone remember
fire, earth, water.
Elemental reckoning—
the earth thunders.

Sharp, sweet spring eddies
through generations, streams
merge in churning unity—
one believer in blood and bone.

Gathering of the Clan

Once a year they
gather to become
kin again   pallets on
the floor   fried chicken
potatoes dripping with
butter   biscuits buttermilk
light   molasses and blackberry jam
fresh from July picking
into the night   lightening in
a jar green glow from
the yard   echoes the old
songs remembered by the walls
ringed by furniture pushed
back for dancing clog buck and
wing   the littlest nodding to
the rhythm of Grandma's heartbeat
one-and-two swing your
partner   new wives still
throw back their heads to
laugh to tunes first fiddled
when outlawed pipes hung
silent in the rafters   rising blood
sings like wind through
autumn maples   bright tartan
swinging to the rhythm
dies into the night.

Flying Bird

Of an evening, rainbows of remnants
spilled across the deep, cool porch,
a beam of memories, the spectrum
of our genealogy. Templates in hand,
Great-gran demonstrated the necessity
of precision and adherence to pattern.

Promised to sister, our ancestral silver
thimble winked in the long, gold light.
Brother and I cut careful patches, not permitted
pricking our fingers in the sisterhood of stitchery.
Though sister's fingers flew nimble,
her feet ran itchy, the template confined.

The legacy winks on my right
hand, brother's children join with mine,
new patches on the long lit porch,
harvesting the rainbow of my scrapbasket,
the pattern of the template unbroken, bating
one block, set out of kilter, remembering sister.

Keeping Time

Sweet mown hay tickles
memory to a summer field,
bales like eggs deposited
in careful rows
near the fence line,
Mama's litany of maimings
sufficient to confine my roaming.
Bob Wills' twin fiddles
sing "San Antonio Rose."
Mama washes dishes
with the radio
in a thick July afternoon,
gate swinging time
in the maple shaded
side yard. Dust roils in the wake
of a rusty, rattling truck.
Right on time Red Tom brings
the mail and my Tootsie Roll.
I chew and swing, Eddie Arnold
sings his "Cowboy Song."
Long light, I retreat to the porch,
Daddy bangs open the gate,
the sun sinks into the pond,
drowns afternoon.

Huckleberries

Spread hot August on a biscuit
dark, thick, purple, and sweet,
storm clouds rolling low.

Bleached backbone of the ridge
shimmers as tin buckets
swallow plump berries.

One eye on the bush, one on the rock
lair of scaly, coiled, lightening,
Granny stands guard with a hoe.

We steal the treasure,
make a getaway, untouched,
meet the storm at the head of the holler.

By night, rows of hot August
gleam purple and sweet in a Ball jar
ready for January biscuits.

Hog Killing

November darkness lit
by stoked hardwood. Men
murmur in the barnyard
hands searching for fire. Cauldron
hums, blades sweep on stone. Small
shadows dress behind the woodstove, sudden
shots ricochet the ridgeline, my
dinner falls at their feet.

Country Burial
(Chlodia Dugger Hensley, 1907-1985)

Overalls, faded, pressed,
creased and all buttons done up
over stark white shirts.
They came, hats in hand,
a solemn procession of
sorrowful respect for
one who delivered
their mothers, tended their
sick, shaped their souls on
Sunday school mornings, laid
the cornerstone of the church
overflowing with flowers
from her cuttings. From
deep hollows, ladyslippers
graced the hands that
taught the preacher his
first lisping Psalms, who
rose to read of the
"virtuous woman" wept
instead as they sang to
speed her soul home.

Pap Goes Back to Texas

Young'n, you'll travel around some
before you settle happy.
Pap's last words written
in my journal mock me
here alone with my guitar,
watching a willow tree
sketch sorrow on the sky.

Pap notched a chew of Red Rose
from a plug, tipped his Stetson
against the sun, cocked the slat back
on the sun-warmed barn wall. Silent
these years since his grin twisted
and his face fell, this annunciation
sent me scuttling for my grandmother,
gone slaying weeds in her private Eden,
me charged his guardian.

Like I left him, on two spindly legs,
chin on his silenced chest, heaven-bound
or perhaps back to Texas, where he played
beneath cottonwoods, rode bareback,
chased wagon trains rumbling out of sight,
dragging dust tails, lured him far from Round Rock.

My restless gene comes of Texas stock,
songs carried on fidgety feet, my spirit leaves
before I've gone. At the random opening
of a journal—like cracking the Bible
for answers, Pap speaks,
assures me of a place and home.

Double Wedding Ring

Patches, pieces, remnants, remains
    of dresses that
    took me to school,
    flounced on the playground,
    and waltzed through piano recitals
    have been joined
    with practiced skill.
The same grandmother
    made the dresses
    of calico and cotton,
    pumping the treadle
    in a heartbeat rhythm.
Patches, pieces, remnants, remains
    of dresses my mother wore
    to carry me
    and my childhood
    neatly traced
    by remnant memories,
    join in a testament
    to skill and love.
A gift crafted
    to celebrate my wedding
    and passage beyond
    calico and cotton.

Sorority

Beans, corn, beets, and berries
laid to rest in the catacombs
of deep cellars,
          they unbend.

Frames fetched from smokehouse
replaced by hams, yams wrapped
in the news, gourds all dry,
          they gather.

Baskets dumped, the pile glitters—
tail of a shirt, skirt ripped
on the fence, scraps of a wedding,
          they swap.

Wedding Rings, Flying Geese,
relics, remnants, remains gathered
into beauty, pressed into utility,
          they stitch.

Trunks yield family treasure,
new pieces join the song, patterns
repeat, the grain runs so true,
          I quilt.

To My Welsh Ancestors

The genetic burden of poetry fell
lamentably onto me. No matter
that bardic names—Owen,
Llwellyn, Gwilym, and David—fell
upon the men of my line, colliers
from the bell pits of Swansea,
cousins to wild Dylan, drunk
on wine, rhyme, and the
grandeur of his own voice.

Their poetry was of invective
and curse, long, linear, multisyllabic
damnations that peppered
their targets like buckshot.
My sire could spin one malediction
for fifteen cruel minutes—red
faced, sweat-popped, hate strangled.

The women crept meek, spoke
platitudes, coaxed beauty from dirt,
manna from dust. The tepid gene
took a twist within the mandala
of my DNA and began to speak.
Once loosed, rhyme and verse
swarmed round, spells chanted
against curse and fist.

Raising the Nap

Spiny, rock-hard pod, seed spent,
the teasel, that early blooming
roadside attraction, brief spring blush,
peaks early, stands hardened,
thorny to lush summertime.

Medieval weavers and fullers
employed the teasel to fluff
and finish, raise the nap,
render the wool chillproof,
watershedding, impenetrable.

My father was my teasel.
His early beauty casually spent,
to our public shame,
we shared him with many.

I became tightly wrapped,
chillproof, acid-shedding,
impenetrable. His venom
and fists rolled away.
I was fulled and teaseled,
nap raised against the elements.

The Fall of the House

The furnace roars, hums, and grinds
coal wormed through the screw feeder
of the stoker. Christmas cedar smells sharp
like bush-hogged fields of late summer.
I sleep with Mama, terrified by the House of Usher
on our weekly movie night. Brother
curls on the other side, fists clenched against
the horrors of the dark. I am wakened
by wheels on gravel and by Daddy's key
in the lock. Mama mutters under her breath
and meets him head on. Sharp words hiss,
the clink and clatter of the kitchen follow.
Three days absent, he smells of smoke, perfume,
and something wild I cannot name, something old like
blue mud along the creek where crawfish mound
their homes and ferns drop spores on leaf litter.
Sure we are asleep, he slips his spit-shined shoes and lies
down in his clothes. Brother breathes even,
I match his rhythm. Something pushes
against me, a hand moves over the new breasts
I hate, the only ones in fifth grade, the ones that ruined
my throw from center to home. He breathes ragged
and reaches again. I nuzzle his hand,
then bite down hard. My mouth tastes metal and salt,
he swears low in the bathroom. He stares me down
from the hall. I know he won't hit this time,
his belt won't fly and he won't tell.
This day, we draw our lines. I hold
his glare and spit the blood in his shoes.

Choose Your Weapons

Racking a shotgun can be mistaken
for no other sound. It might mean
crisp quail for dinner or an orchard
cleared of varmints.

Racking a shotgun satisfies
in a way cocking a pistol cannot,
bolting a rifle approaches, heft,
movement and purpose audible.

Racking a shotgun and cool metal
on flesh woke my father the night
I left for good. We neither spoke.
Slide, rattle, snap.

My practiced ease apparent,
his understanding complete.

Revival

Three inches square, color images of prophets,
heroes, a bland, blond Jesus, and a verse.
I learned to read on the back side, the simple
story of the image. Those cards were prized
by pre-television kids, collected and counted
by little blood-washed lambs, the same league
as Maris and Mantle. David was my first love,
his sling held fast as his faith, Goliath
still and crumpled. Our Sunday school class
met in the pews on the left of the pulpit.
Men and women in opposite corners dealt with God,
in clear view of the class my grandmother taught
since their time, when they clutched a crumpled Jesus.
The first Sunday we didn't drive down home,
to that church, I knew my mother was done with God.
I kept Jesus in a box under my bed for years
until my mother, careening too near death,
remembered those cards of her day. I took
Jesus out, brought Him to her,
stuck the cards all around the room where
she slept easy and breathed deep.

Cumberland Falls, Kentucky

A cicada chorus serenaded the procession
to the falls, insistent grace notes as the rosy
Mead Moon mounted the crest of the ridge.
July clung to our skin, we parted the night to view
the moonbow, an iridescent arc, full moon companion
to the thundering falls, that curved heelprint of the Creator.
First a muted murmur, sweet singing came closer,
nuns filed down from the sycamore path, their harmony
antiphonal to the roar. Perched on the edge of the
current-carved cliffs, wimples gleamed
in the moonglow, the wind lifted
their veils in unison, a flock poised
for flight, song of creation in their throats.

Sweet Savour

One Beale Street twilight, we sheltered
a fierce Memphis storm in the Blues city Café,
watched warily as backlit steam and heat snakes shimmied,
dashed only by Memphis Light and Power trucks, dispatched
to reorder life in the suburbs. "Danger Men Cooking!"

warned the menu. Chef Bonnie Mack held court
in a corner booth—his hat an explosion of perfection,
his apron a snow field. A Billy Dee clone commanded
the grill, launched blue clouds heavenward. Tourist, locals,
working girls crowded elbow-to-elbow, foreign tongues mingled

with a backbeat from a club next door. Three holy sisters
clad in new Elvis shirts paused, consulted a guide, waded the snakes
to enter, unperturbed by the sin that oozed, crept, and slithered
about them. Five waitresses, in efficient iambic strut, dispensed ribs,
smoky-dark and sweet. The room united as one,
gave fervent thanks over burnt offerings

Spring, 1991: Reunion

Thirteen small flags at the head table
for country boys who forgot the lessons
of our grammar school days, duck
and cover, safe routes homes, yellow and
black safety signs, fallout shelters with tinned
survival stockpiled beneath city hall.

Boys forgot to duck and cover in dank
jungles and paddies in the rain, endless
rain of incoming fire more immediate than ICBMs
and nuclear rain our parents promised. Two flags
with yellow ribbons mark time for pin point
airstrikers high above an unseen enemy.

Afterthoughts of the baby boom, lost
in the time warp of televised "police actions,"
Viet Nam, Somalia, Haiti, Panama, Iraq, never
declaring it, we wage it well, still singing protest,
never harmony.

Second Semester

An unmarked semester roll
lies waiting to accuse the missing—
the shot up, the knocked up, sent up
state to be locked away. Memories
run the temporal courses
recalling the endless rolls of nameless faces.

Tragic, struggling, battered faces
drift on and off the roll.
Numbered, they take prison courses
in reading, filling in the missing
parts—home holds no memories
but fists and failure—locked up.

Memories of the called up—
proud, stern baby faces
hide sad, kind memories,
write home, bark roll
counts, letters stop—missing,
no more obstacle courses.

Bright eyes aced their courses,
performed on cue, got scholarships up
north, sailed through, never missed
a beat or a question, open faces
hid nothing, topped the roll
in a class of bright memories.

Astigmatic, fuzzy-edged memories—
mediocre, marginal work in courses
suffered, unnoticed but on roll—
restless, stifled yawns, look up
blandly, imagination unfired—faces
hiding talent—inspiration missing.

Prom queens suspiciously missing—
glorious but tainted memories,
ever jealous smirking faces,
shoddy homebound study courses,
dirty diapers piling up.
Dropped quietly from roll.

The new roll accuses the missing,
Their courses forgotten, only memories
Piling up with ungraded papers of nameless faces.

Nine One One

Half-past fractions in October '62,
the season changed. A frenzy
of bells turned teacher's tone to doom.

Onto each desk slid a diagram of safe
routes home. Barring flight, the duck and cover
drill became Pavlovian choreography.

An icon of Bert the Turtle, looking addled,
his Doughboy helmet askew, replaced
President Kennedy above the chalkboard.

Our terror deepened with the reddening
leaves as for a fortnight we ducked,
covered, and cowered under our desks.

Khruschev blinked, November came.
The war grew cold, barbed wire topped
the Wall, only dry leaves fell.

Our brothers sailed away to police Communists.
We swallowed hard as Slim Pickens
rode the bomb into Strangelove's dream.

My lesson plan unfolds in warm
September. Half-past fractions, I recount
duck and cover, safe routes home.

Frightened mothers rush the school,
Duck and cover disciples search the sky
for heavy rain, instead find terror round our feet.

Joan's Song

She had packed her life deliberately
into cardboard better suited
to liquor and bananas.
Her new space burgeoned
with boxes, lamps, and memories.
Subtle guilt permeated
drapes and carpets abandoned
by other transient lives
confined to three
rooms and a mildewed bath.
A dinner dish he hated went
well with the wine—sweet freedom—
he refused to drink.
She bathed in solitude,
tried a new scent—Confidence—
surprised to find it drove
smudges of guilt from
drapes and carpets abandoned
by other transient lives.
Only then did she take
them down to hang her own.

Remnants

After reading "3a.m. and the Stars Were Out"
by Ron Rash

The vet slides from his truck, rubs his back,
surveys the farmstead, knows the reason
for the dark morning call that waited
too long for Nature to right herself for free.
Foreclosure lurked, insurance against
tangle of barbed wire, body, and shotgun
left me orchard, house, and pasture.
With a look that knew, but knew better
than asking, the sheriff puzzled a cautious
man finding such a clumsy end. My larder
filled by the proceeds of apple butter, honey,
and cheese for the subdivided city folk of the old
lower pasture. We work close in the lamplit stall
to soothe and comfort my best young cow.
His scratchy wool shirt smells of soap, wood smoke,
and leather—man scent remembered.
Hair curls over his shirt collar that misses a button,
his woman grown weary of late calls, overdue bills,
and bartered fare. Firm and gentle, a quick twist
releases a knobby calf to the straw. He lingers
over coffee and checks one last time on
my garden seed and tractor payment that wobbles
for his mama. He crunches down the gravel drive,
stops on the crest of the hill. I see his outline perch
on the tailgate, gaze upward. I imagine he unwraps
the fried pies I left in the seat and pity the woman
who left such hands and a man who stops
to watch the stars graze in the heavens.

Monuments
(for Leatha Kendrick and all Amazons)

Rodin reigned triumphant in Raleigh.
The Dog Star and millennial sun rose
together, broiling queues of faculty wives,
art patrons, schoolgirls, retirees, and I-40
stragglers who caught quick notice on
billboards posted among the orange and white
construction barrels. Among the latter,
we sought respite from August.

A morgue of marble body parts arrests me. Mistress
Camille Claudel emerges again and again from stone,
head, face, torso, hands templates of feminine
perfection: *Aurora* rose gently from a rough, round belly
of marble. It was there I saw your face, your
marmoreal elegance, the warm glow of creation just below
the surface, easy to imagine the chicory blue of your eyes.

A hand here, your face there, a breasted torso
transplanted to create new beauty. The narration
speaks of sculptural marcottage, *reuse of parts created
by the maker*. I wish this for you. Bring perfection
to a new form, discard that which no longer serves you,
chemicals burn sheen to patina and permanence,
a medical marcottage, a fierce surgical artistry.

May your will become the force, the telling of the invasion
your work, the strength of the fight your opus.

Chronology of a Dreamer

Lee Smith: " ...what would you do if somebody
told you that you weren't allowed to write anymore?"
Lou Crabtree: "Well, I reckon I'd just have to sneak
off and do it."

Woolgathering, mama called it.
Get that wash out, quit staring
at them hills. I'd sneak and do it
through the galluses of the overalls
and flapping feed sack sheets.
Stuck a book in my bucket those
hot berry-picking days. I'd read
it on the far side of a briar patch,
on hot huckleberry mountains.

———————

Mooney-eyed my man called it.
Where's my cornbread, been staring
at them hills all day? That baby's
just spoiled...quit petting it so.
Stuck a book in my basket those
herb-picking days on the ridge.
Wildflowers marked the small
stones of short lives. The man
wandered off to another holler
to daddy a passel of farm hands.

———————

Bookish, the others called it,
keeping school for children
I couldn't have, the writing of my sly self
became my letter to the world—

how a bookish woman saved her soul—
standing waist-deep in the hard life,
the books brought me to shore.

———————

Rough hands tender my book
to me. I sign it to a sister
and know if I couldn't write,
I'd have to sneak and do it, she'd
have to sneak and read it,
our souls roam the dark hills.

Nocturne

I'm easing into old age, need less sleep,
which is fine, for the heat of creation
rises in my breasts, burns in my throat,
paints sheen on my skin, wrests me from sleep.

At the purpling of evening, I note
the pileated pair that pecks and preens,
circles the dead Locust, returns to
their careful-pecked, rectangular roost.

My skylight frames the Hunter arching over
with his club and bright belt, his dogs follow.
The Moon, already sunk in the West, pulls the tides
of my body less and less, no longer rules my rhythms.

My mug-warmed fingers wait dawn to blaze
across the ridge, my morning hymn
written by birds on wires, staff and notes
black on the blazing page, moving melody.

Soon the Seven Sisters and Bull rise,
I creak into bed, chase dreams, know
the Hunter stands guard in the South
and lies down in the dawn as I rise to sing.

Diamond Jenny

Diamond Jenny #1

I cried when he left
for the night shift
almost as bad as when
he left for the war.
I was a baby with a baby
and tramps sneaked about
mustard-burned, mean and useless.

"Ol' Blue's in the yard.
the shotgun's loaded.
I been afraid, over there.
Down deep in them holes,
French mud
sucked at my soul.
I'll bang my lunch bucket
on the fence post.
You'll know the footsteps
are mine."

Baby cried and fretted
my dread for me.
One July-thick night
the gate creaked a warning.
I listened, hearing only
boot heavy steps,
a messenger marching
in time to the death-bell
from the mine mouth
tolling casualties,
deep in Kentucky mud.

Diamond Jenny #2

In my Geography book,
I once saw a picture of half a pyramid.
In the cold half-light of January,
My mind wondered
And wandered across the Nile.
I followed the shafts
Running at all angles
To vast chambers,
To small nothings.

The pharaoh was laid,
Still and tar-covered,
At peace in the heart
Of his man-made mountain,
His soul far-gone across dark rivers.

Miss Atkins smacked my hand for daydreaming,
So I forgot the pyramid.
That picture still comes to mind
When I look at the big, granite mountain
That swallowed my father.

Diamond Jenny #3

He enters the arms
of the earth,
darkness embracing him.
Outside, the day begins anew.
The small death,
the daily interment,
unbroken, unnatural cycle.

Leaving the body
of the earth,
he gasps for the freshness.
Outside, the day dies away.
The small escape,
the daily birth,
unbroken, unnatural cycle.

Diamond Jenny #4

Mistress Mine

He spends his day-nights
moving within her darkness.
She, rounded and beautiful,
older than memory,
larger than our lives,
dangerously moist and deep,
like all women keeps her secrets,
her treasures
tucked way, deep inside.
Her hold on our lives
is complete.
My days and nights are filled
with waiting
and the fear
she may someday choose
not to return him
to me.

Diamond Jenny #5
Pound River, 1959

Slick, shiny, and black
like seals,
they floundered, bobbed in eddies
among black, torrent-tumbled boulders.
Child eyes, wide in the cushioned
world of the Ford
wondered at boys sliding,
clean and blond,
into the river,
bobbing up shiny black,
slicked like seals
by coal dust.
"Oh! Why does their mama
let them play there?"
"Don't stare!"
scolded mother,
born of that place,
"It's the only river they have."
The light changed,
descent from the mountain continued.
But child eyes
visioned forever
boys—slick, shiny, and black
like seals—
floundering, bobbing among
black, torrent-tumbled boulders.

Diamond Jenny #6

Always before going under
he gasps as if he might never again.
The mountain looms
gray and scarred above him.
Only Brother Barnes' God and His angels
could look from their Heaven and see
more than he sees spread in the valley below.
Going down, the gasping
gives way to measured labor.
Like the worm in his lunch apple
he crawls through the belly of the mountain,
already halfway to Hell.
(Could have gone to college over at Berea,
but Brother Barnes said only the Devil's work
went on over there.)
His rumbling belly sends him crawling backward
toward food and the chance
to straighten the back
that really won't straighten anymore.
The belly of the mountain
suddenly rolls and rumbles.
On the surface, she belches
like a beer-joint slut.
He and the worm hang
suspended in her belly,
already halfway to Hell.

Diamond Jenny #7

For Silas House

The county agent
feels more than hears
blasting from Jenny #8,
thinks of his children wading
cool, green creeks beneath
slippery shale cliffs, prays blast
schedules be safely memorized.

Days when rain drums
the canvas Jeep cover,
he hears rain pounding large
leaves and white herons
shrieking like tracer
fire across humid heavens.

Lesser of evils, skulking
jungles instead of bending
to mines or raising a crop
of Yankee young'ns in Detroit,
the GI Bill brought him up
sampling soil and replanting
stripped slopes where his
children play in cool, green creeks
upstream from black water.

Cosmic Possum

How We Became Cosmic Possums
(Suburban Appalachian Baby Boomers)

Caught between Country Club and 4-H,
Neither shrimp nor crawdad,
Neither hip nor hillbilly,
Neither feedsack nor cashmere.

Neither shrimp nor crawdad,
Daddy punched the time clock,
Neither feedsack nor cashmere
Worked weekend tobacco on Grandpa's farm.

Daddy punched the time clock,
First generation out of the holler,
Worked weekend tobacco on Grandpa's farm,
Saved for our college diplomas.

First generation out of the holler,
Veterans who never spoke the horror,
Saved for our college diplomas,
Television lullabies shaped weary dreams.

Veterans who never spoke the horror,
Stanley thermos and lunch pail full,
Television lullabies shaped weary dreams,
Believed our country always right.

Stanley thermos and lunch pail full,
Feared beatniks, hippies, and Communists,
Believed our country always right,
Scorned unions in the plant.

Feared beatniks, hippies, and Communists,
Secretly applauded our highest draft numbers,
Scorned unions in the plants,
Wars they never spoke of, fierce dreams.

Secretly applauded our highest draft numbers,
Searched the skies for nuclear rain,
Wars they never spoke of, fierce dreams,
Built fallout shelters for our future.

Searched the sky for nuclear rain,
We learned to "duck and cover,"
Built fallout shelters for our future.
Became the hippies our fathers feared.

We learned to "duck and cover,"
Neither shrimp nor crawdad,
Became the hippies our fathers feared,
Caught between Country Club and 4-H.

The Cosmic Possum Ponders
A Dream of Hunting Rabbits

The last of November rustled down
and graveled dust roiled in our wake
as we drove to the homeplace, to the fields
of rabbits. Not quivery, soft bunnies, noses
twitching, but powerful rabbits, the random
rabbits of thought that spring up from folded
laundry, freshly graded papers, or carrots
chopped for winter stew. Rangy, flea-bitten
rabbits, flushed from dry sage grass in shale
fields too fallow to hold rattling corn skeletons
shivering in the wind. Rabbits that bounce
from scrub cedars to honeysuckle thickets
and briar-tangled warrens, laughing
under their breath at clomping
bipedal pursuit. *My Celtic lineage*
remembers a rabbit hunt symbol
of kenning, a quest for spiritual power.
In my next dream, I will turn away,
feigning sleep, hope they nest in my hair.

The Cosmic Possum
Contemplates Love Poems Lost

Love poems stick just
behind the ballpoint
on my pen. To confuse
them, I tried
typing. They, of course,
refused to be caught
in such a silly way.

I caught some—once—
with a pencil on the
inside cover of a
book of philosophy.
Short of cash, I sold
the book, both the
logic in Descartes
and the passion forgotten.

They run ahead,
always in sight
but too fast to be
captured by the likes
of me. Still I see them
pink, fluffy, lavender,
and mauve racing
among the wooded glades
pursued by sleek ballpoint
and clumsy keyboard,
their virtue still intact.

Finding Herself in Knoxville, Tennessee On a Non-Football Saturday, The Cosmic Possum Visits a Poetry Slam

"Appalachian poets," said the Brier,
"there's one behind every fence post."
Jack Daniels, Blue Ribbon and Heineken
called forth the Muse. Gloom, despair
and agony stirred up like scum
from the pond bottom, squatted center stage.
Misery, like kudzu, twined up the rafters,
brought down the spirit. Yuppie
glossolalia, redneck zenolalia, baptized
in the spirit of verse,
they verb-handled!

Daughters of Necessity

Cassandra

Songcatcher
Cecil J. Sharp (1859-1924)

Sheriff Dugger fetched the songcatcher
just after supper. The last long, gold
light of Midsummer's Eve lit
the path along the well-worn trace.

In the pretty talk of those old
"love songs," the Englishman asked Daddy
to sing; the root seeking the branch, song
of heath and highland, ballad of hill and hollow.

Daddy took down his bow and spun
a night-web. Songcatcher penned
the song to the page, a soot-speckled
snowfield, butterflies pinned in a case.

The songcatcher's lady caught
swift words, a swallow in flight,
snatched the sweet old words
from the honeysuckle moonlight.

Sun rose on Gypsen Davey riding away
with the lady, Daddy sung dry, strong
coffee, sweet milk, sorghum and biscuit,
manna on the dew-sparkled morn.

Felix Culpa

Too wet to plow, we climbed
the ridge where Jack-in-the-pulpit
and Fire pinks fringed woods' edge.

Spent of love, he lay crucified
across my Garden Path quilt, hat low
on his brow to shade the sun.

Stretched beside him, I thought his feet
the prettiest I ever saw on a man. Upright,
they framed the wet bottomland below.

Blue veins traced a mystery map
to his toes. I wiped them with the long towel
of my hair, woke him to adoration.

A cast of hawks rose on a draft
towing spring in their talons,
snaring us in a greening spiral.

I think of those elegant feet,
boot-shod, mud-logged, entrenched
below shell-plowed, fallow fields.

Summer fades, no word comes, I soon
harvest what he sowed before following war.
Tiny feet beat sad tattoos under my heart.

Preacher calls me Magdalene. I refute
him, knowing her wiser in her choosing,
blessed by loving, not damned.

Genesis

My feet washed in yellow-flecked
life water, I set upon the path a woman
trudges alone. Pain crouched near,
stalked me, a breathing thing, a ragged black
beast I mounted and rode through dark valleys,
up ragged peaks, around abysmal ledges
until the burgeoning beast bolted from
under me, tore free, and I fell back
into the light, two instead of one.

Paradise Regained

When I laid down in love
and got up in shame, they sent me
to my aunt in Charleston. Hot,
ripe, and fetid, the over-bearing
green pressed me into myself.

Of an evening, I learned to take
the breeze on the widow's walk,
the rolling blues of the harbor
cooled my eyes, allowed me
to stretch, unfold, breathe.

Storms approached, sent the ocean
rolling like a procession of ridges,
on and on until I believed I stood
on the mountain where my kin slept,
the wrinkled ridge and valley blue,
purpled, and frothy with dogwood.

In the rising night, the moon glittered
on the swells like a cold blue
Hunters' Moon on first frost,
dark shadows mimicked inky deep hollows.
I kept vigil until the gale drove me below.

I packed my grippe, left but
a note. The preacher will condemn,
the whispers burn and scald,
I listen only to the mountains
that called me home.

A Society of Women

The mule took no notice of autumn
shouting from the maples, drifting
from the sycamore by the creek.
The wagon labored up the mountain.

Hats in hand, neighbors begged my pardon
for bringing death. My own sweet mama
brought to bed too old, a sister babe
laid in my arms, a milk goat trailing the wagon.

Mama's great trunk, the babe, the goat—
these Daddy sent before he deserted,
pursuing the sun. A fiddle, a drink, a dream
his only companions west.

The remnant of my own ruin clings to my skirt,
curious of the babe. The preacher's long looks
tell me what I already knew of men. "Just once
before I go to whip the Kaiser," Joel begged.

Queen Anne, cohosh, and Joel
failed to deliver me from shame,
my guilt borne alone, caught
by a granny at midnight.

Preacher's exhortations for my salvation
still ringing from the hillside, men quit us.
As my mother's solemn eyes seek mine
from within my arms.

My Mother's Trunk

plagues me, squats
black in the corner,
clutches cold remnants.

———————

From Richmond town, brought down
by train, schoolmarm,
scholar, believer,
nitpicker, woodchopper,
huddled thin bodies
nearer the pot-bellied
stove. Latin, Shakespeare,
Walter Scott, Milton,
Bulfinch's mythology sink
to the bottom, time only
for spellers, grammars,
arithmetic—the seeds—
their flowers early bitten.

———————

Wild highland tunes
first fiddled when forbidden
pipes hung silent in
the rafters stirred blood
and bone, fierce invocations
lured her heart from books
and chalk to the high
ridge and a fiddling man,—
primrose and bramble entwined.

———————

She wore ashes-of-roses
and wildflowers to wed,
Bible inscribed with seven
generations of begats and
their begotten, tiny high-button
shoes not fit for the ridge,
put back for a time
that never came.

A woman brought
too old to bed—the fiddler
her undoing—cherished
my first crooked stitches
on a nine-patch, a copper
curl matches the braid
on my shoulder, lace
I could not trace, needle
rusted in its tangled
nest. Shakespeare,
Milton, Walter Scott,
Caesar's Latin, and myth
see candlelight the first
time since the primrose
rambled to the ridge. In
their yellowed margins,
elegant copperplate script
reveals the schoolmarm
of the valley. A broken bow
and broadside ballad penned
his fiddling to the page, sang
her siren song.

———————

I re-order her life
with more care than her man's
mournful haste, lay aside
her book of recipes and herbs,
intending a tonic, finding
a cure. Safe from prying eyes
and rough fingers, its margins
her journal, elegant scraps
tucked between pages,—
my letter for finding.

———————

My mother's trunk
consoles me, squats
black in the corner,
embracing our lives.

Coronation

Spring storm recedes, draws crackling
air in its wake, an electric bridal train.
Nape hair prickles, sweet air hums thick
with bees. Holding close the skep, I rest
against an oak sapling, bees loop long
spirals, draping the tree, the skep, the keeper.

Bathed in bees, veins pulsing with wing beats,
time spirals, spring burgeons, buds, swarms.
Settling the skep, I bait the bees with
old honey, last year's comb. One by one,
they seek the sweet until the last, a long
elegant queen, enters to wing-beat applause.

Thalia

Pack Horse Librarian

The earliest of birds have not stirred
and the old rooster dreams of dawn
when I saddle the rented red mule.
A faint fingernail of moon scratches the ridge.

Altair, Deneb, and Vega announce summer
on high though chill pierces my jacket.
Clouds roll dark, Redbuds will riot against
a galvanized sky by dawn boiling up crimson.

My packs bulge with words to be carried
up dark hollows, down steep ridges, through swift creeks.
A scrap of oilcloth, a grateful gift, will keep damp April
from precious papers, bold pictures, worn covers.

Perhaps bright Jenny will tote a babe.
It rode low on her a fortnight ago, ladies magazines
for company, her man building for the CCC,
great western dams his legacy.

Just dawn, a pair of towheads
wrapped in a quilt wait creeekside
swap picture books for warm cornbread
savored slow. The sky bleeds across the ridge.

Mule foot and trail-memory sure,
we make two more stops before April
seeps into my coat, bites my fingers, stings
my eyes, Redbud Winter falling hard.

Carry the books, WPA pays a dollar a day
and all I can read for the coal oil I can spare.

Great Expectations

A chimney with no smoke signed
distress for Jenny, who most often greeted me
from her high porch, bi-weekly visits welcome
interruption from solitary expectations, her man gone
West to work. Inside, Jenny lay sweat-soaked,
hair blazed across the pillow. Laboring the night,
she knew I'd come on my book route. Unburdened and slapped,
the mule headed home, a hasty note to my mother
who soothes women in their need. The re-kindled cook stove
warmed Jenny's feet, for spring lay hidden in fat, chilled buds.
Water boiled, fire flicker reflected in her loosened braids,
I read soft from Dickens to ease her mind, relax her body
to give up the babe. We walked slow circles
on vinegar scrubbed floors, round clean news-covered walls,
letting gravity pull the tide. Near dark, I heard the mule
on the trace, bearing Mama and her black bag of relief.
Swift, firm kneading turned the boy, who came in a gush
with a topknot of flame. Motioning for the Bible,
she declared him Roosevelt, noted the day,
soothed his wail and kissed him Pip
for a poor boy with a happy end.

Jubilation

The fiddled hymn wailed and mourned
down the creek. Blind John leaned
into the music, pulled his heart's
grief through the keening strings.

They churched me, mourned John.
Sour Saul's gone to preaching damnation.
Called me the Devil's harper. I pointed
to Jubal—father of jubilation and them
that harp and flute. Heathen Jews and
infidels, Saul shouted. Pushed me out the
door without my stick. The Lord lead
me home, none came to help.

I recounted my Aunt Cecelia's marvels
of grand cathedrals—fiddles,
oboes, and tall pipes rising
to the vaults like slim poplars
to sunlight, singing to heaven.
I sang a Bach aire Cecelia taught me.
He felt it on the strings, sent it
gliding down the bubbling creek.

I read him Psalms of David—
praise upon strings. He rested,
bathed in sunrays, hoary halo
credited my belief that God denies
pursed lips and pinched hearts,
delights in joyful noise.

Deep Winter

for Silas House

The dark solstice sleet stings,
December sketches glittering glyphs
on a slate sky. Silence falls easy, settles
at snow start. Snow has a sound,
I know this. It begins as quick spiders
on fallen leaves, starched curtains stirring.
Then snow becomes soft wings,
moth applause, blossom-rain
on orchard grass. Heavy feathers
of stern snow pile in resolute rows
by fence rail and frosty road. Bare limbs
shake loose their covers as sibilant evening
stirs, stretches, and sighs, the sound
of snow lost to the wind.

Lydia

Come October

On this mountain, come October, frost is sudden.
The sickle moon reaps a quick kill,
abrupt turn from long, gold days and faultless
crystal skies. Finding my warm shoes, I come
 to a start, not recognizing the feet below me.

"These aren't my feet," she complained
as I massaged and flexed them, dough risen
smooth, or raisin wrinkled in response
to diuretics that rescued her drowning heart.

My hands aren't my hands, these fire-lit days.
Settling to the fire to piece and mend,
her blunt fingers, pink palms, knuckles hinting
at the arthritic knots they will become, ever
busy at a stitch or seam, hang from my arms.

My hands and feet remember the pull
of seasons. Thick hickory bark and tough
corn shucks command them "stack more wood."
Low August fogs whisper "cut more patchwork."
Bare-limbed dogwoods, thick with gaudy
jewels, call "clean the chimney."
My mothers made busy against winter:
tightened boards, filled cellars, strung
hams like macabre ornaments on smoke
dark beams, bundled against the chill
to note that some mother's hands have
replaced and passed their hands onward
in the essential progression of seasons.

Daughters of Necessity

As a girl, I kept company with the Fates,
played in their shadows, fashioned their castoffs
into naïve art, watched them roll yardage
from long, loomed bolts, taste fabric with their fingers,
measure and cut, reworking woven patterns.
They modeled the art of patience, the practice
of perfection, necessity of time unfolding, me,
the reticule of their wisdom. Thread, lint, and errant
needles, no bigger than thorns, clung to their bodices;
like a trail of breadcrumbs, marked their passages.
I feel the Fates measure me each time I cut,
pull out minute stitches they would not approve,
hear them murmur in the whisper
of needles through cotton.

First Day Photo

Summer closes, hot gardens contained
in sparkling rows, mowers soon parked,
windows soon shuttered against endless outside
chores. First day pictures, a bottle-thick squint
into August dew shine. Fifth grade awaits a cornsilk
ponytail poised to bounce just so. The stiff
J.C. Penney three-for-ten dollar shirtwaist indicts
an early puberty, white Keds sparkle, fresh
Blue Horse binder with a zipper pocket,
three hand-sharpened pencils, and virgin white paper peek
from beneath a battered Agatha Christie, her summer best friend.

Red brick heaven waits, chalk dust her perfume,
multiplication a mantra, a world she wants to rule
when the new century turns her timeline. The
town mill wants her, escape route blocked by early
marriages, a steady wage against mama's old age, dervish
machines winding out threads of Fate. Many grill
orders, dirty dishes, and milk cows stand
along the fits and starts journey to the kingdom of the
mind. No hair nets, no uniforms, no punch
clocks, no gold watches for brown lungs, just dreams of
clean boards, new books, and fresh faces when summer closes.

Labor Room

My focal point was to be a photo of Mt. Mitchell,
sparkling, crown of the Smokies, windswept, cool, imperial.
Transition came swiftly and my muscles wrenched
my view to the squat, stone church across the street.

A stout red door, hinged with forged
iron stood against the world, a heart in the
granite façade. The lacquered finish pulsed
a stoplight until mid-summer glare shone hot.

The heart stood firm. Cleansing breath, count
—six hinges, six bolts each—round and round
I counted, breathed, thought of Jesus,
His flaming heart suffering on Sunday School walls.

Lensless and myopic, I rolled onto the lit
and mirrored center stage, the heart
imprinted behind my eyelids until I
delivered in that windlowless theater.

They stripped the doors of red, now glowing
warm with old oak. Each time the light
arrests me on that corner, I count the bolts,
think of God's own heart and my morning of creation.

Phototropism

Visitors congregate in this room of windows,
floor to ceiling canvases of the seasons.

At fifty, the light easily finds me here
with my cotton patch stretched tight across a white
pine hoop with a tension Torquemada would envy.

Wide, refurbished chair arms balance the cotton patch,
my thimble winks in the north light as I trace
rows of color across the frame.

My journal crouches alongside, the random rabbits
of thought that spring up, startled from the
cotton patch, caged there, wide-eyed, quivering.

Music for my mood twines round the incense
of strong, brown coffee, whirled by lazy overhead blades
in this room of light and making.

Winter Garden

November washes the last leaves
from the Pin Oak, tosses the last
of the acorns down the graveled drive.
Leaden clouds dim
the light to submarine gray.

Fingers restless, my workbasket near,
I crave growing a new garden
of patches. November bears down.
Muttering wind spits sleet at the
windows. I spread fabrics across
my table, jewelled jams and jellies,
taste and savor them with my fingers.

I pluck and trim, knot and tie,
the cotton garden blooms, spills
out of my lap, basks in the fireglow.
My plot for the winter, the patch
garden grows, gathered and bound,
becomes sustenance against the cold.